Ragnar Lothbrok

The Saga of a Viking Warrior King

CW01497346

Hourglass History

Contents

Chapter 1: The Birth of a Legend

In the wind-tossed wilds of the North, during an era draped in the cloak of mystic folklore and heroic tales, a legend was born. A formidable figure of history and lore whose deeds would sear his name into the annals of time. This is the saga of Ragnar Lothbrok, the Viking warrior king.

We begin our journey in the late 8th century, an age characterized by its harsh yet profoundly beautiful environment. The Norse world was a canvas of unending forests that whispered secrets to the wind, daunting mountains that pointed their snow-capped peaks towards the heavens, and raging seas that could as easily give life as they could claim it. Amidst this breathtaking panorama, a new saga was ready to unfold – a saga that was as untamed and gripping as the land itself.

Ragnar was born into a world that was perpetually wrestling with the juxtaposition of creation and destruction. It was an era where the gods themselves were said to walk among men, their whims as capricious as the northern winds. Our protagonist was no ordinary child; his lineage traced back to the formidable king, Sigurd Hring, a man renowned for his prowess in battle and sagacity in governance. Born of royal blood, Ragnar was immediately thrust into a world of privilege and expectation. Yet, these early years were more than just a birthright; they were a crucible that would forge him into the legendary figure he was destined to become.

Growing up in the Viking settlement was akin to being thrown into a whirlwind of traditions, customs, and rites that were as old as the gods themselves. The settlement was not merely a collection of wooden longhouses nestled amidst the wild landscape. Instead, it was a living, breathing organism that pulsed with life. The clamor of craftsmen perfecting their trade, the smell of roasting meat and baking bread, the echo of laughter and songs filled the air, creating a cacophony that was as intriguing as it was inviting. This was Ragnar's childhood soundscape – a symphony of human resilience and tenacity against the relentless onslaught of nature.

Viking children, regardless of their lineage, were expected to learn the skills necessary for survival from a very young age. The brutal northern climate showed no mercy to the ill-prepared. From the moment Ragnar could walk, he was taught to respect the land, to listen to its whispers, and to comprehend its silent warnings. The seemingly endless forests surrounding the settlement were not merely trees and undergrowth; they were a source of fuel, a provider of food, a haven for wildlife, and a spiritual link to the gods themselves.

Each day was a lesson in survival, interspersed with tales of heroism and valor. The sagas, told and retold over generations, were the moral compass guiding every Viking. They spoke of gods, monsters, and men – tales of bravery, cunning, and strength. As a young boy, Ragnar would huddle with others around the crackling hearth as the village skald, his voice a mellifluous melody in the silent night, spun tales that made the gods seem within arm's reach. Ragnar's eyes, reflecting the flickering flames, were full of youthful awe and reverence. He lived those tales, those battles, those victories, and defeats. With each passing saga, a seed was sown in his heart – a seed of dreams, of aspirations, of a life that mirrored the heroes of old.

In many ways, Ragnar's childhood was a reflection of the Viking ethos – robust, resilient, and fiercely independent. Yet, it was also marked by the unique complexities of his royal lineage. As the son of a revered king, he had a legacy to uphold, expectations to meet, and a role to play in the larger tapestry of the Norse world. The weight of his lineage was as much a privilege as it was a burden. It was this delicate balancing act between personal aspirations and societal obligations that would lay the foundation of the saga that was Ragnar's life.

Ragnar was not merely born; he was shaped, sculpted by the potent forces of nature and nurture, his destiny irrevocably tied to the pulse of the world he inhabited. He was a product of his time, a reflection of his environment, and a symbol of a culture that left an indelible mark on the annals of history. His saga was a testament to the indomitable spirit of the Vikings – a spirit that braved the fury of the seas, the wrath of the gods, and the trials of existence.

This, then, is where our saga begins. At the birth of a boy whose name would resonate through the ages. A name that would become a legend. Ragnar Lothbrok. Through the lens of this singularly captivating figure, we traverse the intricate pathways of the Viking era, navigating the intricate interplay of history, mythology, and human resilience. Our saga begins here, not just the saga of a man, but the saga of a people, of an era, of humanity itself. For to know Ragnar is to know the Vikings, to understand their ethos, their beliefs, their indomitable spirit.

This chapter thus marks the beginning of an epic journey, a voyage through the annals of time, with the Viking warrior king, Ragnar Lothbrok, as our guide. It is a journey that promises to be as tumultuous, as exhilarating, and as unforgettable as the man himself. And so, let the saga unfold. Welcome to the world of Ragnar Lothbrok. Welcome to "Hourglass History: Ragnar Lothbrok - The Saga of a Viking Warrior King."

Chapter 2: Life in a Viking Settlement

In the rugged landscape of Scandinavia, where the elements of nature clashed in a furious symphony of earth, sky, and sea, the Viking civilization blossomed. It was here that young Ragnar Lothbrok spent his formative years, learning the skills and customs that would shape his future as a legendary Viking warrior king. To comprehend the man, we must first understand the society that molded him. The cradle of his life, a Viking settlement, was more than just a cluster of thatched houses; it was a microcosm of the Viking world, pulsating with a potent mix of everyday reality, mythology, and cultural complexity.

The day began with the first hint of dawn, as the blush of the morning sun painted the horizon. The settlement, with its longhouses constructed from stout timber, started humming with life. Here, nestled between the untamed wilderness and the temperamental sea, the Vikings made their homes. The architecture of these longhouses was not a frivolous design choice; it was a strategic adaptation to the hostile climate. Built long and narrow with sturdy wooden beams and roofs made from layers of thatch, these houses were designed to withstand harsh weather, retain warmth during the chilling winters, and provide space for communal living.

Within the longhouse, life revolved around the central hearth, a symbol of home and hearthfire, where food was cooked, clothes were dried, and tales were spun. This fire was a lifeline against the unforgiving cold of the Scandinavian winters. Aromas of roasting meat, fresh bread, and smoked fish would mingle in the warm air, the heart of the home, providing sustenance and comfort.

Around the bustling heart of the home, daily life took shape. Women, often underestimated in their role but every bit as crucial as their male counterparts, busied themselves with chores like cooking, weaving, mending clothes, and tending to children. These women were the heart of the Viking settlements, their labor often unsung but indispensable. They managed the household, oversaw the dairy and brewery, cared for the animals, and taught their children essential skills. This was the world Ragnar's mother navigated daily, a world defined by a mix of strength, care, and wisdom.

Parallel to this domestic sphere, men engaged in various activities. From tending to the fields and managing livestock to building ships and crafting weapons, Viking men honed their skills for survival and exploration. Young boys, including Ragnar, were expected to contribute, their childhood a constant cycle of learning, observing, and doing. These tasks, initially seen as chores, were in reality the first steps towards becoming a Viking warrior. For a young Ragnar, these activities were not mere duties; they were an initiation into the intricate world of Viking adulthood.

The settlement was alive with more than just the rigors of daily life. It was a vibrant social structure bound by a unique system of laws and rights, the Althing. This assembly of free men and women met to discuss matters of importance, settle disputes, and make decisions that impacted the entire community. This democratic aspect of Viking society provided a glimpse into the essence of their societal structure – egalitarian, with a strong emphasis on justice and order.

Amidst the hustle and bustle, the skalds or poets had a special place in the Viking settlements. They were the storytellers, the keepers of tradition, and the mouthpiece of the gods. As dusk fell, and the crackling fire cast long shadows on the faces of the gathered Vikings, the skald would begin to weave his magic. As the rhythmic cadence of his voice echoed in the silent night, sagas of gods, heroes, and monsters came alive. To the young and impressionable Ragnar, these stories were not mere tales; they were lessons of honor, bravery, cunning, and strategy – an education no conventional learning could impart.

Amidst this interplay of work and leisure, the settlement offered more than just a habitat. It was a self-sufficient entity with farmland for crops, pasture for livestock, and nearby forests for hunting game and gathering timber. The fjords and sea offered ample fish and means of transport, which later played a crucial role in the Vikings' naval dominance. Theirs was a society intimately linked to nature, and their survival was a testament to their ability to use the resources around them judiciously.

To grow up in such an environment was to learn resilience, adaptability, and a profound respect for the balance of life. For young Ragnar, this settlement was his first playground and his first battlefield. Here, he first learned to swing an axe, sail a boat, follow the stars, and listen to the whispers of the old gods in the rustling leaves.

Life in a Viking settlement was, therefore, not a mere existence; it was a vibrant dance of survival, community, and identity. It was here that Ragnar Lothbrok, the boy, began to take on the mantle of Ragnar Lothbrok, the legend. Every aspect of life in the settlement shaped his path, imparting the skills, values, and beliefs that would become his guide in the adventurous saga that lay ahead.

In the next chapters, we will follow this path, tracing the steps of Ragnar as he evolves from a young boy in a Viking settlement to a warrior, explorer, and eventually, a legendary king. But for now, let's take a moment to appreciate the humble beginnings of this Viking hero, in the bustling settlement that bore witness to the birth of a legend.

Chapter 3: First Blood

In the burgeoning dawn of his life, Ragnar Lothbrok was more than a boy born into a Viking settlement. He was the flame that danced upon the northern winds, the echo of ancient legends in the making. Yet, before his name would thunder through the annals of time, the first pivotal moment of his life unfolded: his first battle, his first taste of the warrior's path. The saga of Ragnar Lothbrok, the warrior king, truly began with this inaugural spillage of enemy blood on the canvas of his destiny.

The morning air was sharp, spiked with the scent of cold iron and muted excitement. As the red-gold rays of dawn stretched across the horizon, the heart of the Viking settlement pounded with the drums of war. Ragnar, though still a youth, was to join his first raid, an initiation into the violent ballet of Viking warfare. Every nerve within him thrummed with a strange combination of anticipation, fear, and exhilaration. His muscles coiled tightly, his grip tightened on his axe, and he saw the world through the fevered lens of the imminent combat.

Raiding was the fiery vein that ran through Viking society. For a people whose lands were harsh and often unyielding, the lure of the sea, with its promise of distant shores filled with untapped resources, was irresistible. Plunder was a practical necessity, a means of survival. Yet, it was also a cultural rite of passage, a demonstration of courage, and a path to wealth and reputation. As the longships knifed through the frigid waters, carrying Ragnar towards his destiny, he could almost taste the salty tang of the adventure that beckoned.

The target was a nearby settlement. Disputes over territory, resources, or honor often resulted in these local conflicts, the microcosm of the larger battles that the Viking Age was known for. As their longship grounded on the unfamiliar shore, Ragnar stepped into the battlefield for the first time. The world around him seemed to narrow, his heart pounding in his ears, his vision focused on the approaching enemy.

The first clash of battle was a chaotic storm. Men roared, steel sang its deadly tune, and the air was filled with the scent of sweat, blood, and primal fear. Ragnar stood in the heart of this storm, his world slowing as if trapped within the grasp of a winter's chill. Then, he made his move.

His opponent was a burly man, a seasoned warrior, who must have seen the young newcomer as little more than a nuisance. Yet, as Ragnar moved with the swift unpredictability of a winter gale, the man's overconfidence became his downfall. The dance of combat was not merely about strength; it was about agility, cunning, and relentless will, lessons that had been instilled in Ragnar since he first held a wooden training sword. As the man lunged, Ragnar sidestepped, his axe swinging in a wide arc to crash into his opponent.

The blow was not fatal, but it drew first blood. The sight of the red liquid staining the snow-filled ground was a stark moment of realization for Ragnar. He had stepped across a threshold from which there was no return. He was no longer merely a youth of a Viking settlement; he was a warrior in the making.

The battle raged on, a whirlwind of violence and primal fury. Yet, within this storm, Ragnar found a sense of clarity. Every dodge, every parry, every strike became a step in a deadly dance that he was starting to understand. As the day bled into evening, the battle ended with the Vikings emerging victorious.

The return to their home was marked with celebration, songs of victory echoing through the frosty night. Yet, for Ragnar, the celebration bore a different taste. It was not merely a celebration of victory, but the acknowledgment of his passage into the warrior's path. He had tasted his first battle, spilt his first blood, and felt the raw, unyielding call of warfare that would become a constant companion in his life.

In the grand tapestry of his life, this first battle was but a single thread. Yet, it was the thread that would lead to the weaving of a warrior, a leader, a legend. Ragnar Lothbrok had drawn his first blood, a crimson testament to the path he was destined to walk, a path that would etch his name into the annals of history and legend. His saga, the saga of a Viking Warrior King, had truly begun.

Chapter 4: The Warrior's Path

The initiation into the dance of death was over, and the young Ragnar had tasted his first victory. Yet, this was merely the beginning, the first step on a path littered with battles, conquests, and tales of unmatched valor. Ragnar Lothbrok was now poised to tread upon the path of the warrior, a journey that would mold him into the legendary figure celebrated in sagas and songs.

In the land of the Northmen, the line between life and warfare was not merely blurred but often non-existent. A Viking's existence was deeply entwined with the art of combat, his status in society dictated not only by his lineage but also by his prowess in battle. It was this life that beckoned Ragnar, the life of a warrior that was as rewarding as it was perilous.

After his first raid, Ragnar threw himself into his training with renewed vigor. Each day, the young Viking would spar with his kin and fellow warriors, honing his skill and learning the language of battle. The art of fighting was more than just physical strength; it was an intricate dance of strategy, speed, agility, and mental endurance. Ragnar's every waking moment was dedicated to mastering this dance, from handling a variety of weapons to learning how to read his enemy's movements and intentions.

Each weapon was a tool, an extension of the warrior himself. The axe, in particular, was a favored weapon among the Vikings, and Ragnar was no exception. He learned to wield it with skill and precision, its sharp edge singing tales of upcoming victories. Alongside it, he mastered the use of the spear, the sword, and the iconic round shield that was as much a weapon as it was a form of defense. Each weapon was an instrument in the symphony of war, and Ragnar was learning to play them all.

Yet, Ragnar's training did not merely involve weapons. He learned to navigate the treacherous terrain of their homeland, using the landscape as both a shield and a weapon. He became adept at swift and strategic movements, understanding when to attack, when to hold back, and when to wait for the right moment to strike.

His skills were not limited to one-on-one combat. The Vikings were renowned for their use of formations during battles. Among them, the shield-wall was the most famed, a tactical formation where warriors would stand shoulder to shoulder, their shields interlocked. It was a sight to behold, a living, moving wall of iron-clad determination. It was a tactic that Ragnar would come to use time and time again, a testament to the power of unity even in the face of overwhelming odds.

Over the years, Ragnar's reputation grew. He was no longer seen as a mere youth but as a warrior to be reckoned with. He was bold, yet not reckless; strategic, yet adaptable; a fearsome opponent and a reliable comrade. Yet, this path was not merely about personal growth; it was a reflection of the Viking culture and its deep-rooted belief in bravery, honor, and the relentless pursuit of glory.

Indeed, the warrior's path was not merely a career or a way of life; it was a destiny. For the Vikings, the ultimate honor was to die a warrior's death in battle and earn a place in Valhalla, the hall of the slain in Asgard, where they would feast and fight until the end of days. It was this belief that drove Ragnar and his kin to risk their lives in raids and battles, their hearts aflame with the promise of eternal glory.

In the grand saga of his life, these early years on the warrior's path were a transformative period for Ragnar. He was not merely shaping his own destiny; he was stepping into the role of the quintessential Viking warrior, a figure revered and feared in equal measure. He was becoming a part of a legacy that would outlast him, his actions echoing in the annals of Viking lore.

Yet, even as Ragnar tread upon this path, he understood that being a warrior was not merely about mastering the art of war. It was also about leadership, about earning the respect of his comrades, about making difficult decisions in the heat of battle. He was not merely a fighter; he was a leader of men, a role that carried with it a weight and responsibility that he was willing to shoulder.

This was the warrior's path that Ragnar chose to walk, a path that required sacrifice, courage, and an unyielding spirit. It was a path that would take him from the familiar shores of his homeland to far-off lands, through countless battles and bloodshed, through victories and losses. Yet, Ragnar Lothbrok did not shy away from this journey. Instead, he embraced it, each step etching his name deeper into the annals of history and legend.

By stepping onto the path of the warrior, Ragnar had accepted the call of destiny, a call that was echoed in the clash of steel, the roar of battle, and the silent promise of glory. He had become a part of a grand legacy, a saga that would be retold time and again, his name synonymous with bravery, leadership, and the relentless spirit of the Viking warrior.

In the grand tapestry of his life, this chapter marked Ragnar's metamorphosis from a young Viking into a seasoned warrior. Yet, this was merely the beginning. The path of the warrior was long and winding, its end shrouded in the mists of time. And as Ragnar walked this path, he would come to realize that every battle was a story, every victory a verse in the grand saga that was his life.

Indeed, Ragnar Lothbrok had stepped onto the warrior's path, his heart aflame with the promise of glory, his spirit resolute in the face of adversity. And as he tread upon this path, he was not merely forging his destiny; he was also shaping the destiny of his people, leaving a legacy that would echo through the annals of history and legend. For this was the saga of Ragnar Lothbrok, the saga of a Viking Warrior King.

Chapter 5: Saga of a Seafarer

The land of the Northmen, with its rugged coasts and icy fjords, was a land born of the sea. For a young Viking like Ragnar Lothbrok, the call of the ocean was irresistible. The sea was a world unto itself, promising adventures, spoils, and the unparalleled thrill of the unknown. As he embarked on his seafaring exploits, Ragnar was about to immerse himself in the complex, yet rewarding art of navigation, turning the vast, untamed ocean into his personal realm.

It was not uncommon for Vikings to become skilled seafarers. Indeed, their reputation as fearless explorers and daring raiders was built upon their impressive naval abilities. Yet, seafaring was not just about battling the waves and steering the ship; it was a delicate dance with the elements, requiring a deep understanding of the sea, the weather, and the stars above.

Mastering the sea's dance meant learning its rhythms and moods, its ebbs and flows. It was about reading the color of the water, the direction of the waves, the flight patterns of the seabirds, and the delicate dance of the sea creatures below. It was about understanding the whispers of the wind, the scent of the salt in the air, and the subtle changes in the temperature. Ragnar, like all Viking mariners, was not merely a warrior or a raider; he was a seer of the sea, a reader of the waves.

Navigating the open sea was a complex task that required more than just intuition; it required a keen understanding of the celestial bodies. The Vikings, despite their seemingly rough demeanor, were adept at reading the skies. They relied on the sun, the moon, and the stars for direction. They had a deep knowledge of the night sky, understanding the movements of the stars, and using them as a map, a celestial guide leading them through their seafaring journeys.

The importance of celestial navigation cannot be understated in the context of Viking expeditions. The Vikings were known to use primitive but effective instruments like the sun compass, a device that allowed them to use the position of the sun to determine the cardinal directions. Ragnar, like all adept Viking seafarers, would have been well-versed in these techniques, using the sky above as his guide as he navigated the waters below.

Ragnar's seafaring skills were not just about navigating; they were also about managing and leading a crew. As a leader, he was tasked with maintaining order, ensuring the well-being of his men, and making strategic decisions during their expeditions. Each journey was a test of his leadership skills, his ability to inspire, and his capacity to maintain morale in the face of the relentless sea.

Another crucial aspect of Ragnar's seafaring saga was the Viking ship itself. These vessels, with their elegant designs, sturdy structures, and practical features, were a testament to the Vikings' remarkable shipbuilding skills. Their ships, often termed as 'longships', were made for speed, agility, and flexibility. They were designed with a shallow draft, allowing them to navigate both deep sea and shallow waters, a feature that made them particularly effective during surprise raids. The ship's prow was often adorned with intricate carvings, with designs ranging from animal heads to mythical creatures, a symbol of the Vikings' artistic sensibilities and their religious and mythological beliefs.

Ragnar, as a seasoned Viking warrior and a growing leader, would have been well-versed in managing these vessels. His understanding of his ship's structure and mechanics, its strengths and weaknesses, would have played a vital role in his seafaring exploits. His ship was not just a vessel; it was a trusted comrade, a part of his seafaring saga.

The saga of a seafarer is a tale of battles, not just with other men, but with the sea itself. It is a tale of courage in the face of the relentless ocean, of resilience against the raging waves, and of the indomitable spirit of exploration. Ragnar Lothbrok, in his journey on the warrior's path, embraced the saga of a seafarer, weaving an intricate narrative of adventure, leadership, and naval prowess.

Through these seafaring exploits, Ragnar Lothbrok etched his name deeper into the saga of the Vikings. Each journey was a testament to his skills as a navigator, his abilities as a leader, and his spirit as a Viking. His saga was not merely a series of adventures; it was a tale that embodied the essence of the Viking spirit, a spirit born of the sea and guided by the stars. A spirit that danced with the waves, braved the storms, and sailed into the heart of the unknown, for the love of exploration, the thrill of the raid, and the promise of glory. The saga of Ragnar Lothbrok, the seafarer, was just beginning.

Chapter 6: Lagertha, the Shieldmaiden

Ragnar Lothbrok, the seafarer, the warrior, the raider, was a man of the sea and the battlefield, a man of courage and cunning. Yet, his saga was not solely of his deeds and feats. Interwoven in his story was a woman of equal courage, a shieldmaiden, and his first wife, Lagertha. The tale of Lagertha is as mesmerizing and complex as the man she stood beside. She was a force unto herself, a woman who defied societal norms, a woman who picked up the shield and sword, a woman named Lagertha.

Lagertha, as the sagas narrate, hailed from Norway. Her origins were humble, her beginnings seemingly ordinary, yet her spirit was anything but. Her character was marked by strength and resilience, a flame that was kindled in the face of adversity. The sagas narrate a brutal episode from Lagertha's early life where her settlement was ravaged by a vicious earl, leaving her and other women in a state of subjugation. It was in this darkness that Lagertha's flame started to flicker and grow, her spirit undeterred by the horrors around her.

In this time of despair, the sagas sing of a young, audacious Viking from Denmark who heard of this dire situation and made his way to Norway. This Viking was none other than Ragnar Lothbrok. A fight ensued between Ragnar and the malevolent earl. Yet, Ragnar did not battle alone. Standing shoulder to shoulder with him was Lagertha, a woman who refused to remain a victim. She fought alongside the men, her courage unrivaled, her strength unyielding.

Ragnar was undeniably drawn to Lagertha, not just for her beauty but for her bravery and prowess in battle. It is said that Ragnar was so taken by Lagertha's spirit that he sought her hand in marriage, to which she agreed. Thus, Lagertha and Ragnar's paths intertwined, their destinies now one.

As Ragnar's wife, Lagertha did not confine herself to traditional roles. She did not cast her warrior spirit aside, but instead, she held onto it, proving time and time again that she was a warrior in her own right. Lagertha was a 'shieldmaiden', a woman who chose the path of a warrior. These women were revered figures in Viking society, seen as embodiments of the fierce Valkyries from Norse mythology.

Riding on horseback, charging into the heart of the battle, Lagertha stood her ground, her shield held high, her sword ready to strike. She fought with the strength of a hundred men, her spirit matching the fierce winds of the North. As a warrior, she was as formidable as any man, her skill in battle matched only by her strategic mind.

Her relationship with Ragnar was a partnership in every sense. They stood as equals, their respect for each other rooted in their shared courage and warrior spirit. They battled together, their swords striking as one, their shields standing firm. In the eyes of Ragnar, Lagertha was not just a wife but a comrade, a fellow warrior, and an irreplaceable part of his saga.

Yet, their relationship was not just defined by their shared battles. Lagertha and Ragnar had three children, two daughters, and a son. Their family life, though interspersed with the tumult of battle and adventure, had its moments of peace and affection. Lagertha, though a warrior, was also a mother, her love for her children as fierce as her spirit in battle. She raised her children with the same strength and courage that she brought to the battlefield, nurturing in them the spirit of the Vikings.

Their lives together, however, were not without strife. The sagas tell of the complexities and challenges that marked Ragnar and Lagertha's relationship. Through their trials and tribulations, through their moments of joy and sorrow, Lagertha and Ragnar's story remains a testament to their characters, their resilience, and their undying spirit. Their love story, much like their individual tales, was not of peaceful tranquility but of fiery passion and enduring resilience, a love that was forged in the heat of battle and weathered the storms of life.

Lagertha's story does not end with her time as Ragnar's wife. She carved out her own path, her own destiny, her own saga. But, that is a tale for another time. For now, we honor Lagertha, the shieldmaiden, the wife of Ragnar, the woman who fought alongside men, the woman who refused to be a victim, the woman whose courage ignited a flame that could not be extinguished. Lagertha, a woman as legendary as the man she stood beside, a woman who was, in her own right, a Viking legend.

Thus, as we traverse the saga of Ragnar Lothbrok, we must pay homage to the women who played integral roles in his life. Lagertha, the first wife of Ragnar, a woman who held her own, is one such figure. Her life, her spirit, and her deeds serve as a testament to the strength and resilience of Viking women. A testament to the Viking belief that courage and honor were not the sole domain of men, but qualities that both men and women could possess.

The saga of Ragnar Lothbrok is as much about the women in his life as it is about the man himself. These women, with their strength and spirit, added depth and dimension to Ragnar's tale. As we delve deeper into the life of Ragnar, we continue to honor these women and their contributions to the legendary saga of Ragnar Lothbrok, the Viking Warrior King.

Chapter 7: The Dragon's Teeth

There are deeds that define a man, and then there are deeds that elevate a man to the realm of legends. For Ragnar Lothbrok, the Viking Warrior King, slaying a dragon was one such deed. This exploit, remembered and retold in whispers around the fire and shouts in the mead halls, marked a pivotal moment in Ragnar's saga. Yet, the tale is not merely one of victory against a monstrous foe; it speaks to the core of who Ragnar was as a man and as a leader.

The creature that Ragnar faced was no ordinary beast, but a dragon, or more accurately, a gargantuan serpent named Jörmungandr. In the Viking lore, dragons and serpents held a special place, representing immense power, wisdom, and imminent danger. They were seen as insurmountable challenges, encounters with the divine and demonic. Therefore, when the saga speaks of Ragnar facing Jörmungandr, it signifies an encounter with a force beyond human comprehension.

But how did Ragnar, the Viking warrior, come face-to-face with this mythical creature? The sagas reveal that the serpent was causing chaos in Ragnar's realm, laying waste to his lands, threatening his people. It was a danger that could not be ignored, a challenge that needed a hero.

Ragnar, rising to this daunting challenge, showed not only his physical prowess but his cunning intellect. He understood that facing the beast with brute force alone would lead to certain death. Instead, he opted for a strategy that utilized his understanding of the beast and his expertise in crafting and using equipment.

He ordered a suit of clothing to be made, unlike any other. This was no ordinary fabric but bore the roughness and resilience of the wildest elements of nature. It was woven from the wool of the hardiest sheep, boiled in pitch, rolled in sand. The result was a garment thick and rough, one that could hopefully withstand the serpent's venomous assault.

Ragnar's weapon of choice was a spear, but not a standard one. This was a weapon forged for a specific purpose, with a head designed to pierce the thick scales of the beast. The spear was blessed in rituals, its purpose sung to the gods and the spirits of the ancestors, asking for their guidance and blessing.

Thus equipped, Ragnar set out to confront the beast. His journey to the serpent's lair was one fraught with tension and apprehension. The land bore the marks of the serpent's wrath, fields scorched, homes ruined, the air thick with the stench of fear and destruction. But within Ragnar, there was no room for fear, only a steadfast determination.

The confrontation between Ragnar and the serpent was one for the ages. The sagas tell of a battle that shook the earth, a clash between man and beast that seemed to defy the natural order. Ragnar, in his rough clothing and armed with his special spear, stood against Jörmungandr, the embodiment of chaos and destruction.

The battle was fierce and grueling. The serpent attacked with venomous fury, its breath poisoning the air, its body thrashing and coiling with lethal force. But Ragnar stood his ground, his clothing shielding him from the worst of the venom, his spear ready to strike.

In this battle, Ragnar was not merely a man but a symbol of the indomitable Viking spirit, facing the odds with courage and determination. His every move was calculated, his every strike a blend of power and precision.

In the end, the saga tells of a victorious Ragnar, standing over the fallen beast, his spear piercing its skull. The earth shuddered, a silence fell, and then arose a victorious roar. Ragnar had slain Jörmungandr, the chaos-bringing serpent. He had protected his people, defended his lands, and proved his worth as a leader.

This victory was more than just a physical triumph. It was a testament to Ragnar's strategic intellect, his courage, his relentless spirit, and his dedication to his people. He was no longer just Ragnar, the warrior; he was Ragnar, the dragon-slayer, the protector of his people, a man of legend.

Ragnar's triumph over Jörmungandr reverberated throughout the Viking lands, etching his name into the annals of their history. It marked him as a hero, a leader, and a legend. His story was told and retold, his deeds praised, his name hailed.

Thus, the tale of Ragnar's encounter with the serpent, his victory against the odds, serves as an emblematic narrative in the saga of the Viking Warrior King. It showcases the true essence of Ragnar Lothbrok, reflecting his strength, cunning, courage, and dedication. It reaffirms his status as a legendary figure, one who stands tall in the grand tapestry of Viking lore.

Yet, we must remember that sagas, as captivating and evocative as they may be, often weave a mix of fact and fiction. The encounter with Jörmungandr is more metaphorical than literal, likely symbolizing a significant challenge that Ragnar overcame. However, the core essence of the tale, the characteristics it attributes to Ragnar, remain relevant and tell us much about the man, the leader, the legend.

Whether it was a serpent of epic proportions or a challenge of another kind, what remains unquestionable is that Ragnar faced it with the heart of a warrior and the intellect of a king. And in doing so, he became more than a man; he became a legend, a symbol of Viking courage, tenacity, and resourcefulness. His tale, his saga, thus continues to resonate, echoing through the corridors of history and across the expanse of time, a testament to the enduring legacy of Ragnar Lothbrok, the Viking Warrior King.

Chapter 8: Power and Politics

In the annals of Viking history, the rise of Ragnar Lothbrok is a tale worthy of the grandest sagas. A humble warrior he may have begun, but his path would lead him to power beyond any Viking's dream. And yet, his rise was not only the result of his martial prowess and legendary exploits; the political structure of the Viking world played a significant role in shaping his destiny. In this chapter, we delve into this world, unraveling the intricacies of Viking politics and leadership and understanding how Ragnar ascended to the hallowed seat of a king.

To truly understand Ragnar's rise to power, one must first comprehend the societal and political framework that the Vikings operated within. The Vikings did not have a unified kingdom; rather, their society was divided into numerous independent clans and tribes. These groups were scattered across the Scandinavian territories, each with its own chieftain or jarl at the helm.

These chieftains were warriors first, their position earned not by bloodline or divine right but by the strength of their arm and the respect they commanded among their followers. They led their people in battle, made decisions for the welfare of their tribe, and represented them in the larger assemblies known as 'things'. These gatherings were integral to the democratic process of the Viking society, where matters of law, disputes, and leadership were openly discussed and resolved.

The title of 'king' in Viking society was not a monarchical one as understood in the modern sense. Viking kings were more accurately over-chieftains, jarls who wielded influence and control over multiple clans and territories. Their status was not necessarily hereditary, often earned through strategic alliances, victories in battle, and the personal loyalty of other jarls. Thus, when the sagas speak of Ragnar Lothbrok as a king, it signifies a man of immense influence and power, one who commanded the loyalty of numerous jarls and their clans.

Ragnar's ascent to power must be contextualized within these societal norms and structures. His journey to kingship was not a linear one, rather, a trajectory shaped by personal accomplishments, strategic alliances, and an intuitive understanding of the political dynamics of his world.

His dragon-slaying feat, as explored in the previous chapter, marked him as a hero and protector, earning him respect and admiration far and wide. Yet, Ragnar was not content with resting on these laurels; he understood that true power in the Viking society lay in the hands of the jarls and kings.

To this end, he worked on forging alliances, using his renown as a warrior and dragon-slayer to win the support of other chieftains. Ragnar's charisma and leadership qualities played a crucial role in this endeavor. He was a man who inspired loyalty, not through fear or coercion, but through respect and admiration.

Ragnar also knew that his military accomplishments were key to consolidating his power. His exploits, like the victorious raids and his strategic acumen, made him a valuable ally and a formidable foe. This military prowess, coupled with his diplomatic efforts, gradually expanded his sphere of influence.

An essential aspect of Ragnar's rise was his capacity for strategic marriage. In Viking society, marriages were often used as a tool to cement alliances, strengthen bonds, or expand influence. Ragnar's marriages to Lagertha and later Aslaug were not merely romantic endeavors but strategic decisions that consolidated his power and expanded his influence.

In time, Ragnar's influence grew so expansive that he was recognized as a king, an over-chieftain commanding the loyalty of multiple jarls and their clans. He had successfully navigated the complexities of Viking politics, using his strengths and opportunities to ascend to a position of unrivaled power.

However, the politics of power are a tricky business. Ragnar's position brought with it not only authority but also responsibility and danger. As a king, he was now tasked with the welfare of numerous clans, their disputes, their ambitions, their loyalties. He had to balance the needs of his followers with the realities of Viking society, often a complex and demanding task.

Moreover, a king's seat is always a coveted one, and Ragnar was no exception. His power and influence invited envy and rivalry, often from unexpected quarters. The sagas speak of numerous challenges to his rule, battles fought not only on the fields but within the halls of power. Ragnar's story, therefore, is not just a tale of ascent but also of survival, of a man navigating the turbulent waters of power.

In the final analysis, the story of Ragnar Lothbrok's ascension to power is a tale of ambition, strategy, and resilience. It offers a window into the political world of the Vikings, a world where power was fluid, leadership was earned, and politics was a game played with swords and marriages alike. It underlines the fact that Ragnar Lothbrok was not just a legendary warrior but also a shrewd politician and leader, one who left an indelible mark on the political landscape of the Viking world.

Chapter 9: The Blood Eagle

In the annals of the Vikings, few rites are as terrifyingly vivid as the ritual of the Blood Eagle. Enshrined in their legends and sagas, it stands as a stark testament to the raw brutality of their warrior culture. According to the sagas, it was a rite Ragnar Lothbrok himself is said to have invoked. To comprehend the significance of this ritual in Ragnar's narrative and Viking society, we must unravel the layers of myth and mystery that surround it.

As the sun broke through the mist over the fields of Aelle, the defeated King lay helpless, his fate sealed. All around, the Vikings were celebrating, their jubilant roars echoing off the fjords. In their midst stood Ragnar Lothbrok, a cold determination in his eyes. He had a promise to fulfill, a debt to be repaid in blood. The Blood Eagle awaited King Aelle.

The Blood Eagle was not an everyday ritual, but rather, a ceremonial execution reserved for the most hated of enemies. It was a statement, a public display of dominance, vengeance, and utter disdain. Its gruesome process served as a testament to Viking ruthlessness and their concept of poetic justice.

According to the sagas, the condemned was laid prone, his hands and legs bound. The Viking executioner would then slice open the back of the victim, hacking through ribs until they splayed outwards, resembling bloody wings. In some renditions, the victim's lungs were pulled through the open wound, draping them over the rib-wings to complete the grotesque spectacle.

To the Vikings, the Blood Eagle was not just an act of physical violence; it carried profound symbolic and religious overtones. The eagle was a potent symbol in Norse mythology, associated with Odin, the Allfather, and god of war and death. By carving an eagle onto the back of a fallen enemy, the Vikings were ostensibly offering their foe's spirit to Odin, a visceral, bloody sacrifice to their chief deity.

This act was particularly poignant in the case of Ragnar and King Aelle. In Viking society, honor and vengeance were deeply intertwined. When an insult or injury was dealt, it was not only expected but required that the wronged party seek retribution. Failure to do so would result in loss of face and respect. Aelle, having incurred Ragnar's wrath, was marked for the ultimate retribution – the Blood Eagle.

By invoking the Blood Eagle, Ragnar was making a statement. Aelle's life was not enough; he sought to annihilate his enemy's honor and memory. It was a calculated act, designed to send a clear message to friend and foe alike about the consequences of crossing Ragnar Lothbrok.

It's critical to remember, however, that our understanding of the Blood Eagle comes from the sagas and chronicles, passed down through generations, often rich with hyperbole and poetic license. Archaeological and historical evidence provides no concrete proof of the ritual's existence, leading to spirited debate among scholars.

Some argue that the Blood Eagle was a literal event, a harsh reality of the Viking world. Others propose that it was a misunderstanding, a mistranslation of the original Old Norse texts. Yet another school of thought suggests that it was purely metaphorical, a gruesome image crafted by skalds, the Norse poets, to emphasize the brutality and finality of a Viking's revenge.

Regardless of its factual authenticity, the Blood Eagle holds significant symbolic value in the saga of Ragnar Lothbrok. It encapsulates his ruthless warrior ethos, his sense of honor, and his unforgiving pursuit of vengeance. It stands as a stark symbol of the power he wielded – the power to judge, to condemn, and to exact the most brutal of reprisals.

The Blood Eagle also provides a stark contrast to the Christian traditions of mercy and forgiveness that were slowly encroaching on the Viking world. In Ragnar's time, these two cultures, Norse and Christian, were colliding in increasingly violent and transformative ways, shaping the course of history in the process. Through the lens of the Blood Eagle, we gain a deeper understanding of this cultural clash, a theme that echoes through the rest of Ragnar's tale.

The story of Ragnar Lothbrok and the Blood Eagle is one of power, vengeance, and stark brutality. It is a testament to the world in which he lived, a world where power was etched in blood and honor was worth dying - and killing - for. As we delve deeper into Ragnar's life, the shadow of the Blood Eagle looms large, a potent reminder of the ruthless code that guided him and the violent era that shaped him.

Chapter 10: The Viking Raid on Paris

Dark were the waters of the Seine as they reflected the pallid light of the moon. The typically lively trade route bore an unusual stillness, disrupted occasionally by the distant howling of a wolf or the nocturnal rustling of the woods. That was until the silhouette of an ominous fleet emerged from the vast expanse of darkness.

It was Easter in the year 845 when Paris awoke to the sight of an imposing fleet of 120 Viking longships, led by a man whose reputation had swept across Europe, instilling fear in the hearts of many – Ragnar Lothbrok. This event marked the first of many Viking raids on Paris and is one of the most notable episodes in the saga of Ragnar Lothbrok.

To understand the importance of the siege and its aftermath, we must first look into the historical context. At that time, Francia was divided into a complex system of duchies and counties, ruled over by the Carolingian dynasty. Paris was not the capital then, but it held strategic and symbolic importance.

As dawn broke, panic echoed through the city. The Frankish army was away, engaging the forces of the rebellious Breton duke, Nominoe. The city's defense fell on the shoulders of the outnumbered and unprepared Parisian militia. They watched helplessly as the Vikings, expert seafarers, navigated the currents of the Seine, their dragon-headed longships bearing down upon the city like a ravenous swarm.

Ragnar was no stranger to the art of siege warfare. His experiences had honed his strategic acumen. Rather than a full-frontal assault, Ragnar chose to besiege the city, cutting off its lifeline – the Seine. The blockade brought commerce to a standstill, leading to scarcity of supplies and a slow, insidious demoralization of the inhabitants. Paris, the jewel of the Seine, was being strangled into submission.

While the siege took its toll on the Parisians, Ragnar's men camped on the Île de la Cité, enjoying their spoils. These Northmen, driven by the promise of plunder and the glory of battle, reveled in their imminent victory. Meanwhile, Ragnar prepared for the final act.

A week later, Charles the Bald, the King of West Francia, arrived with his forces. By then, the city was on its knees. Rather than risking a full-blown conflict with the Vikings, the king chose negotiation, a testament to Ragnar's prowess and the fear it inspired. The Vikings were paid a ransom of 7,000 French livres (around 2,570 kilograms of silver and gold), known as Danegeld, to lift the siege and retreat.

This event was not just a military victory for the Vikings, but a psychological one. The 'ransom for peace' set a precedent, showing that kingdoms were willing to pay vast sums to avoid Viking onslaughts. It also marked a significant shift in

Viking strategy, from hit-and-run raids to large-scale invasions and sieges, validating Ragnar's position as a leader among his people and a terror among his enemies.

The raid had a profound impact on Paris too. It exposed the city's vulnerability, leading to significant changes in its defense architecture, including the construction of fortified bridges and the commissioning of a permanent defense force.

However, despite the terror he wrought and the legacy he left, the historical evidence linking Ragnar Lothbrok directly to the 845 Paris siege is ambiguous at best. While the Viking leader of the raid is often named as Ragnar in popular culture, the primary historical source, the Annals of St-Bertin, simply refers to a "certain pagan Reginherus" or "Reginheri." The connection between this Reginheri and the legendary Ragnar Lothbrok has been made in later years, fueled by similar exploits detailed in the sagas.

The Viking raid on Paris presents a powerful image – a fleet of longships bearing down upon an unprepared city, led by a warrior king from the north whose name would become a byword for terror. It's a chapter from the life of a man who straddled the line between history and myth, an echo from an age of heroes and villains, of honor and brutality, of sagas sung beneath the starlit skies of the North.

The audacious siege of Paris further cemented Ragnar's legendary status, whether or not it was him specifically who led the attack. It was a chilling demonstration of Viking power, of their daring spirit, strategic brilliance, and seafaring mastery. It painted the Vikings not as mere marauders, but as a formidable force capable of shaking the foundations of the great Frankish empire.

In the annals of Viking history, the raid on Paris stands as a testament to their far-reaching influence and a chilling reminder of a time when dragon-headed longships emerging from the mist heralded the coming of a storm. And at the center of this storm, stands a figure shrouded in legend - Ragnar Lothbrok, the Scourge of Paris.

Chapter 11: Gods and Rituals

The world of the Vikings was one intertwined with the spiritual and divine. They revered their gods and ancestors, and much of their life and tradition were intricately entwined with religious practices. Ragnar Lothbrok was no exception, and his life too was guided by faith. In this chapter, we delve into the labyrinth of Norse mythology, drawing from the tales of the sagas and ancient traditions to explore the religious beliefs and rituals of the Vikings, including Ragnar's personal devotion to the gods.

The Vikings were polytheistic, believing in a pantheon of gods and goddesses, each presiding over different aspects of life and nature. Chief among these deities were the Æsir, the primary gods of the Norse pantheon, who dwelt in the celestial fortress of Asgard.

In this celestial abode, Odin, the Allfather, ruled supreme. Known as the god of wisdom, war, death, and poetry, he was often seen as a patron of kings and warriors, who sought his favor before battle. It is said that Ragnar too held a deep respect for Odin, often invoking his name before setting off on raids.

Alongside Odin was Thor, the thunder god, renowned for his strength and valor, and his fierce battles against the giants.

He was the common man's god, protector of the people and the realms, and held an important place in the faith of the Vikings, including Ragnar.

Among the goddesses, Freya, the goddess of love, beauty, and fertility, was highly revered. She was also associated with war and death, welcoming half of those fallen in battle to her hall in Asgard.

Religion for the Vikings was not confined to temples and sacred groves. It was woven into the very fabric of their daily life, their actions guided by a code of ethics influenced by their religious beliefs. They saw the world around them as imbued with spiritual significance, with gods, spirits, and supernatural beings existing alongside them.

The Vikings held a complex belief in fate. Central to this was the concept of the Norns, three mystical beings who wove the threads of fate, influencing the course of events in the world. Vikings believed that each person's destiny was preordained, shaped by the interplay of their actions and the whims of fate. This belief in predestined fate, or 'wyrd', often guided Ragnar's actions and decisions.

Ragnar, like his people, sought to earn the favor of the gods through rituals and sacrifices, known as blóts. These rituals were essential to Viking worship and could range from simple daily offerings to grand ceremonies involving the sacrifice of animals, and sometimes even humans.

During these rituals, the Vikings would gather in sacred spaces, such as groves, temples, or even their own homes. They would feast, drink, and offer their sacrifices to the gods. The most significant of these were the seasonal blóts, held during key events like the start of spring or before major expeditions, which were vital in securing divine favor.

Ragnar, too, is said to have conducted blóts before his raids, seeking the gods' favor for victory. He would offer sacrifices, often of livestock or prized possessions, and make solemn vows, promising further offerings upon his successful return. It was perhaps this deep-seated faith, this unwavering belief in the gods and his fate, that lent him his exceptional courage and charisma.

In addition to these rituals, the Vikings also practiced seiðr, a form of Norse magic associated with prophecy and divination. While it was generally practiced by women, known as völvas, certain men also practiced seiðr. It is unknown whether Ragnar himself was versed in this art, but it is likely that he would have consulted völvas before significant actions or decisions.

The Vikings' view of death was deeply tied to their religious beliefs. They believed in an afterlife, where warriors fallen in battle would join Odin in his grand hall of Valhalla, feasting and fighting until the end of days. It was a belief that fueled their courage in battle and their acceptance of death. Ragnar, too, held this view, his faith a steady beacon guiding him through life and towards his ultimate fate.

In exploring the gods and rituals of the Vikings, we delve deeper into the world that shaped Ragnar Lothbrok. We see a man steeped in his faith, guided by his gods, and shaped by the complex web of rituals and beliefs of his time. It was a world where gods and men interacted, where divine favor could be sought, and where destiny was an intricate tapestry woven by unseen hands.

Chapter 12: Aslaug, the Seer's Prophecy

In the saga of Ragnar Lothbrok, amidst battles and voyages, gods and dragons, emerges the figure of Aslaug, a woman of legend who would intertwine her destiny with that of the great Viking hero. She would become his wife and the mother to his children, her life entwined with his, as woven by the Norns themselves.

Aslaug's story begins not with her, but with her parents, who were figures of legend themselves. Her mother was the renowned shieldmaiden, Brynhildr, and her father, the mighty hero, Sigurd, who had slain the dragon Fafnir. Their union, however, was short-lived, ending in tragedy and deception. Aslaug, their only child, was left an orphan, cast adrift on the tumultuous sea of fate.

Despite such inauspicious beginnings, it was apparent even then that Aslaug was not an ordinary child. Legend says that she was born with the imprint of a dragon's head on her right thumb, a sign of her extraordinary destiny. Her early years were spent in the care of Heimer, a loyal retainer of her parents, who sought to protect her from those who might want to harm the last heir of Brynhildr and Sigurd.

Aslaug's beauty was striking, rivaled only by her intelligence and wisdom. It was said that her hair was as bright as the fields of wheat kissed by the summer sun and her eyes were deep and clear as the purest springs. Yet, her beauty was hidden behind a rough facade as Heimer, fearing for her safety, dressed her in rags and made her appear a beggar to protect her from the greed of men.

The saga tells us that it was in such attire that Aslaug first crossed paths with Ragnar Lothbrok. He came upon her in the Norwegian woods, struck by the girl who seemed out of place amidst the common folk. Intrigued by her uncommon demeanor and intelligent eyes, he asked her to join his household. Yet, Aslaug, ever the clever one, set a condition. She would only join him if he waited for her, promising to come to him "neither dressed nor undressed, neither fasting nor eating, and neither alone nor in company."

True to her word, Aslaug arrived at Ragnar's hall wrapped only in a fishing net, biting an onion, and accompanied by a dog. She had met his conditions in a way he had not expected, showcasing her quick wit and intelligence. Ragnar, already intrigued by her unconventional appearance, was further captivated by her display of wit. He was said to have laughed heartily, his eyes twinkling with admiration and interest. In Aslaug, he found a match for his own intellect, a flame that danced as fiercely as his.

With this, Aslaug entered Ragnar's life, and her story became inextricably linked with his. They were married, and Aslaug bore him many sons, each as remarkable as their parents. Ivar the Boneless, the strategist; Bjorn Ironside, the resilient; Sigurd Snake-in-the-Eye, the marked one; and

Hvitserk, the bold. Aslaug's sons with Ragnar would grow to become figures of legend themselves, each making his mark on the annals of the Viking Age.

However, it was not just as Ragnar's wife and the mother of his children that Aslaug made her mark. She was his confidant and advisor, offering her wisdom in matters both political and personal. Her sharp mind and foresight proved invaluable, helping guide Ragnar's decisions and shaping the destiny of their family.

One example of Aslaug's wisdom can be seen in the tale of their son, Ivar. Upon his birth, it was clear that Ivar was different. He was born with legs as weak as a baby lamb's, seemingly a significant disadvantage in a culture that prized physical strength and prowess. Yet, Aslaug recognized in Ivar a unique strength. She encouraged Ragnar to let Ivar live, foreseeing that his wisdom and strategic mind would make him a great leader. History, as it turned out, would prove her right.

Yet, as in all great sagas, Aslaug's life was not devoid of strife and tragedy. Her relationship with Ragnar was strained over the years, especially after his interest in Thora Town-Hart led him astray. Despite these trials, Aslaug's strength and wisdom remained unyielding, like the prow of a longship weathering a storm.

Her influence extended beyond her lifetime, living on in her sons. The sons of Ragnar, guided by the wisdom and teachings of their mother, would go on to etch their own sagas, the echoes of Aslaug's influence reverberating through their deeds.

In the end, Aslaug's story serves as a testament to the role that women played in the Viking Age. They were not mere bystanders to the deeds of men but were instrumental figures in their own right. They navigated the stormy seas of Viking politics, raised warriors, and left indelible marks on the tapestry of history.

Aslaug's life, intertwined with that of Ragnar, is a saga unto itself. A saga of strength, wisdom, and resilience. In the annals of Viking lore, amidst the tales of heroes and battles, gods and monsters, Aslaug's saga shines brightly, her dragon's imprint a testament to a life of significance, forever entwined with the legend of Ragnar Lothbrok.

Chapter 13: Sons of the Dragon Slayer

The sagas speak of Ragnar Lothbrok's many children, each a force in their own right. Four of his sons are particularly famous: Ivar the Boneless, Bjorn Ironside, Sigurd Snake-in-the-Eye, and Ubbe. This chapter will take us into the life and deeds of these legendary figures, how they carried their father's legacy, and carved out their own paths in the tapestry of Viking history.

Ivar the Boneless

Born of Aslaug and Ragnar, Ivar was known by an unusual moniker, "the Boneless." While there are many theories explaining this epithet, the sagas say it was Aslaug's prophecy that foretold Ivar's condition. Displeased with Ragnar's impatience in their marital bed, Aslaug warned him that their haste would result in a child cursed with weak bones. Ivar, as the result, was born with limbs as flexible as if they were devoid of bones.

Despite this, Ivar's physical weakness was juxtaposed by his sharp intellect. The sagas describe him as a brilliant strategist, using his mind as his weapon. His cunning was said to be instrumental in leading successful raids and outsmarting his enemies, compensating for what he lacked in physical strength.

Bjorn Ironside

Bjorn Ironside, a name that embodied his invincibility in battle, was another of Ragnar and Aslaug's sons. Unlike Ivar, Bjorn was known for his physical strength and bravery. His nickname, "Ironside," was attributed to his ability to resist and survive injuries in battle, as if he was clad in iron.

Bjorn's most famous exploit was his raid on Italy. The sagas recount an audacious ploy, where Bjorn faked his death to bypass the defenses of the Italian city of Luna, making it one of the most audacious Viking raids of that time.

Sigurd Snake-in-the-Eye

Sigurd earned his name, "Snake-in-the-Eye," due to a distinctive mark in one of his eyes, resembling a snake or a dragon. It was said that this mark was a portent of his lineage and destiny.

Sigurd's most prominent story in the sagas is his marriage to the daughter of King Ælla, the man said to have caused Ragnar's death. This union, however, did not bring peace; instead, it highlighted the tension and conflict that the sons of Ragnar would inflict upon Ælla's kingdom.

Ubbe

Less is known about Ubbe, the fourth son of Ragnar and Aslaug. Nevertheless, he was said to be a capable warrior and participated in the raids alongside his brothers. His role in avenging Ragnar's death further highlights his commitment to his family's legacy.

In truth, it is challenging to separate the sons of Ragnar from their father's colossal legend. Their exploits are often told in conjunction with their father's saga, inextricably woven into a shared family legacy. Yet, each of them emerged as unique individuals, their characters and actions distinct and formidable. They inherited Ragnar's courage and resourcefulness, as well as his lust for adventure and conquest.

Through their deeds, the sons of Ragnar were not merely his heirs, but active contributors to his legend. They embraced their roles as warriors, kings, and leaders, each marking the Viking world with their unique stamp. From the British Isles to the shores of the Mediterranean, they spread the legacy of their father, instilling both fear and respect in the hearts of their friends and foes alike.

Yet, it would be a mistake to reduce them merely to extensions of their father. Each son carried their own ambitions, dreams, and personal codes of honor. They were not just sons of the Dragon Slayer; they were men of their own making, their destinies intertwined yet distinct from Ragnar's.

The saga of Ragnar Lothbrok is as much a story of his sons as it is his. Each son represents a facet of Ragnar's personality, his values, and his legend. They carry his legacy forward, their deeds serving as testaments to their father's influence.

Yet, their lives were not without struggles and trials. They had their share of rivalries, both with each other and with external foes. They faced treachery, loss, and hardships. Yet, through these, they rose, their characters tempered, their legends forged.

As the sons of the Dragon Slayer, they lived their lives in the shadow of a mighty figure, yet they emerged from it, each carving out their path. They were the continuation of Ragnar's saga, each chapter of their lives a testament to the enduring legacy of the legendary Viking warrior-king, Ragnar Lothbrok.

Chapter 14: The Great Heathen Army

The saga of Ragnar Lothbrok's sons does not end with their individual exploits. After their father's tragic demise, the sagas tell of a grand mobilization of forces, a swarm of Viking warriors, a monstrosity of Norse might never seen before. They called it the "Great Heathen Army." In this chapter, we delve into this remarkable assembly of Viking power, its composition, campaigns, and the impression it left on the annals of the Viking Age.

Gathering of the Sons

The spark that ignited the creation of the Great Heathen Army was a tragedy - the death of their father, Ragnar Lothbrok. Stories tell of Ragnar meeting his end at the hands of King Ælla of Northumbria, cast into a pit of venomous snakes. Upon hearing of their father's cruel death, Ragnar's sons Ivar the Boneless, Bjorn Ironside, Sigurd Snake-in-the-Eye, and Ubbe vowed vengeance.

But their response would not be a swift and impulsive counterstrike. Instead, it would be an elaborate, calculated gathering of a massive Viking force, one that would shake the kingdoms of the British Isles to their core. Ivar, demonstrating his keen strategic mind, proposed the creation of a great army. Instead of small bands of raiders, they would mobilize a force large enough to conquer. The other brothers agreed, and the gears of war began to turn.

Composition of the Great Heathen Army

The sagas and historical texts differ in their accounts of the army's exact size, with some sources suggesting that it comprised thousands of warriors. It was a grand coalition, a horde of battle-hardened warriors, all bound by the common cause of avenging Ragnar. Men from all walks of Viking society joined the ranks, from simple farmers seeking glory and wealth to Jarls eager to expand their power.

The army was not just a random assembly of warriors but was well-organized and purpose-driven. The four sons of Ragnar—each a formidable leader in their own right—directed the army's operations. Ivar, known for his cunning, was the chief strategist. Bjorn, the embodiment of a Viking warrior, was the inspirational figurehead. Sigurd, with his religious inclinations, acted as the spiritual guide, and Ubbe, the reliable, was the army's steady hand.

Campaigns and Conquests

With their forces gathered, the Great Heathen Army set sail for the British Isles, the lands of Ragnar's supposed killer. They first landed in East Anglia in 865 AD, a place that would serve as their winter quarters and a stepping stone for the invasion.

From East Anglia, they moved to Northumbria, where they sought their primary vengeance. The Army besieged the city of York, a strategic and symbolic target, being the seat of power of King Ælla himself. The city fell in 866 AD, and with it, Ælla was captured. The sons of Ragnar exacted their revenge through the horrific ritual of the blood eagle, a grim reflection of the fate that had befallen their father.

But the Great Heathen Army did not stop with Northumbria. Its ambition was larger; its appetite for conquest insatiable. The Army marched southward, targeting the kingdom of Mercia, which fell to the Viking onslaught in 874 AD. Next, they turned their gaze to the Kingdom of Wessex, ruled by the formidable King Alfred the Great. This campaign, however, was not as successful as the previous ones and marked the beginning of the Army's decline.

Legacy of the Great Heathen Army

Though the Great Heathen Army's campaigns eventually faltered, its impact on the Viking Age and the British Isles was undeniable. It had shown the world the might of a unified Viking force, one that could seize kingdoms, not just raid villages. The Army's activities caused major political shifts in the British Isles, contributing to the creation of the Danelaw, a swath of England under Viking control.

Moreover, the Great Heathen Army signified the Viking transition from sporadic raiding parties to large-scale invasions and settlement efforts. This shift was reflected in the later Viking invasions of France and other regions.

Perhaps most importantly, the Great Heathen Army served as a symbol of filial vengeance and the fulfillment of a duty towards one's blood. It exemplified the Norse code of honor and vengeance, one that required blood to be paid with blood. In seeking justice for their father, Ragnar's sons rallied an unprecedented force that echoed their father's legendary status, reflecting Ragnar's spirit in their actions.

The saga of the Great Heathen Army is a monumental chapter in the story of Ragnar Lothbrok's sons and the Viking Age. It represents the peak of their collective power, driven by their quest for revenge. The roar of the Great Heathen Army has since faded into the whispers of history, but its echo continues to reverberate, a testament to a time when the sons of the Dragon Slayer brought kingdoms to their knees in honor of their father's memory.

Chapter 15: The Legacy of a Legend

As we delve deeper into the intricate web of Ragnar Lothbrok's saga, we cannot ignore the influence his life, and the myths surrounding it, have had on both his contemporaries and subsequent generations. His legacy, blending both fact and fiction, has left a formidable footprint on the sands of time. This chapter will dissect the elements of this legacy, tracing the echoes of Ragnar's life through history.

A Fierce Warrior

Ragnar Lothbrok, even without the layer of myth and legend, was an embodiment of the ideal Viking warrior. His courage, tactical brilliance, and indomitable spirit reflect the Norse warrior ethos, making him a potent symbol of their martial culture.

This aspect of Ragnar's legacy was most potent during the Viking Age. His exploits inspired countless warriors, who looked up to him as the epitome of bravery and martial prowess. He was the shield-bearer they rallied behind, the spearhead they emulated. Ragnar's life was a saga penned in the blood and glory of battles, a narrative that told every Viking that they too could reach such heights of heroism and honor.

King and Leader

The sagas tell us that Ragnar was not just a warrior, but also a ruler. This part of his legacy is layered with uncertainty due to the scarcity of historical evidence. But if the stories hold any truth, then Ragnar's leadership and statesmanship deserve recognition.

As a king, Ragnar exemplified the qualities of strength, decisiveness, and charisma. He held the respect of his warriors, maintained the stability of his lands, and expanded his influence through both warfare and alliances. These achievements paved the way for other Viking rulers to follow, effectively setting the blueprint for effective leadership in the Viking Age.

A Pioneer of Viking Exploration

The Viking era was a time of exploration and expansion, and Ragnar's adventures on the high seas embody this spirit. His supposed expeditions to foreign lands, whether for raiding or exploration, mirror the Vikings' insatiable thirst for discovery and conquest.

Ragnar's voyages, as per the sagas, spanned across the known world, from the British Isles to the distant east. These explorations, whether historically accurate or not, depict the reach and ambition of the Vikings. They inspired countless Viking seafarers, each of whom yearned to leave their mark on distant shores, following the wake of Ragnar's legendary longships.

The Father of Great Men

Ragnar's influence is not only seen in his own life but also in his progeny. His sons, Ivar the Boneless, Bjorn Ironside, Sigurd Snake-in-the-Eye, and Ubbe, are significant figures in the Viking Age. They carried forth his name, not merely as descendants but as bearers of his legacy.

Each son embodied a facet of Ragnar's legend. Ivar, with his strategic brilliance; Bjorn, with his indomitable strength; Sigurd, with his spiritual connection; and Ubbe, with his steady leadership. These qualities did not merely echo their father but also enhanced his legend, cementing the Lothbrok lineage's place in history.

The formation of the Great Heathen Army, as previously discussed, was a direct outcome of Ragnar's legacy. The army was a manifestation of the bond of blood and honor, a testament to the weight of the name Lothbrok. It was a grand declaration of Ragnar's enduring influence, a fierce echo of his roar resounding across the British Isles.

The Birth of a Legend

While the historical Ragnar's life and achievements stand as a monumental legacy, the legend that has grown around him adds another layer to his influence. This legendary Ragnar, part man, part myth, has become an enduring symbol of the Viking Age.

The tales of Ragnar slaying a dragon, his marriages to Lagertha and Aslaug, his countless victories, his tragic death, and the subsequent revenge of his sons, all contribute to a narrative that transcends the boundaries of history. This narrative, immortalized in sagas and songs, has made Ragnar a timeless figure, a symbol of an era marked by bravery, exploration, and change.

Ragnar Lothbrok: The Symbol of an Era

Ragnar's life, both as a man and a legend, has left an indelible impact on history. His influence was not confined to his lifetime but continued to ripple through the ages, shaping the course of events long after he was gone.

Ragnar Lothbrok, as a symbol, embodies the essence of the Viking Age - the courage, the thirst for adventure, the skill in battle, the respect for the gods, and the unwavering spirit. He stands as a beacon, casting long shadows of influence that continue to shape perceptions of the Viking era.

Moreover, the blending of fact and fiction in Ragnar's narrative reflects the intriguing duality of the Viking Age - a time of historical significance and mythical resonance. As we continue to unearth more about this period, the legend of Ragnar provides a compelling lens through which we can explore and understand the world of the Vikings.

As we delve further into the legacy of Ragnar Lothbrok, it becomes clear that his influence extends beyond his life and the lives of his sons. The name Ragnar Lothbrok has become synonymous with the Viking Age, an emblem of a time when dragon-headed longships filled the seas, and fierce warriors penned their sagas in the annals of history. The echoes of his life, real and legendary, continue to resonate, offering us valuable insights into an era that has forever shaped the course of history.

Chapter 16: The Death of Ragnar Lothbrok

Death, in the Viking culture, was not an end but a transition, a voyage from the mortal world to the realms of the gods. The Viking warrior, clad in his battle-gear, welcomed death in combat as a ticket to the eternal mead halls of Valhalla. But how does a legend, a figure larger than life itself, meet his demise? In this chapter, we will explore the many tales surrounding the death of Ragnar Lothbrok, a subject as intricate and controversial as the man himself.

The Warrior's Demise
The sagas are rife with varied accounts of Ragnar's death, each entwining fact, myth, and dramatic license into a complex tapestry. One version, often popularized in visual media and literature, recounts his demise at the hands of King Ælla of Northumbria. The tale is as riveting as it is gruesome, a testament to the brutal reality of the Viking Age.

It begins with Ragnar's ambition to raid the prosperous lands of Northumbria. He sails towards England, not with his legendary fleet, but a handful of ships, fueled by the confidence that has seen him through countless battles.

Upon landing, Ragnar and his men are met with fierce resistance. King Ælla, determined to safeguard his kingdom, leads a formidable defense. In the ensuing battle, the Vikings, outnumbered and overwhelmed, face defeat. Ragnar, captured in the melee, is taken prisoner, his legendary status nothing more than a whisper in the face of King Ælla's triumph.

In an act of vengeance and deterrence, Ælla condemns Ragnar to a horrifying death. He is thrown into a pit teeming with venomous snakes. As the creatures coil around him, sinking their fangs into his flesh, Ragnar faces his fate not with pleas or cries but with a chilling prophecy. He foretells the doom of Ælla, a gruesome retribution to be wrought by his sons. As his life ebbs away, the Viking hero, the legendary Dragon Slayer, succumbs not on a battlefield but a snake pit.

A Legend's Prophecy
Ragnar's grim prophecy would become a significant element in the subsequent saga of his sons. It added a layer of retribution to his legacy, an unfulfilled promise of vengeance. Ragnar, even in death, was a catalyst, his demise not an end but a spark that would ignite the fury of the Great Heathen Army.

Moreover, his dignified acceptance of death epitomized the Viking warrior ethos. There was no fear or desperation, only a calm acceptance, almost an eagerness to join Odin in Valhalla. His final moments were not of a man succumbing to death, but a warrior embracing it.

Ragnar's death, particularly his method of execution, added a layer of martyrdom to his legend. His end was not a warrior's death in battle but a martyr's demise, a concept not prevalent in Viking culture but still powerful in shaping his saga. It added a narrative of injustice, a righteous cause for his sons' impending retaliation, a thread that would run through the ensuing chapters of the Lothbrok saga.

Ragnar's Death: Myth or History?

As with most aspects of Ragnar's life, his death too treads the fine line between history and legend. Did Ragnar Lothbrok, the legendary Viking chieftain, meet his end in a snake pit? Or is it an embellishment, a narrative tool employed by the saga writers to dramatize his end?

The historical validity of Ragnar's death by snakes is contentious. Contemporary accounts of the period do not corroborate this story. They do not even confirm if a figure named Ragnar Lothbrok was active during the proposed time of his death.

Yet, historical accuracy often takes a back seat in the face of narrative impact. The story of Ragnar's death is an undeniably compelling tale, brimming with drama, emotion, and a chilling prophecy. Whether it reflects historical events or is a product of creative imagination is a question that perhaps adds to its allure.

Moreover, the lack of clarity does not diminish the influence of Ragnar's death story. It remains a crucial element of his saga, a turning point in the narrative, setting the stage for the deeds of his sons. The legend of Ragnar's death has seeped into popular culture, epitomized in literature, television, and artwork, a testament to its enduring appeal.

In the grand tapestry of Ragnar Lothbrok's saga, his death stands as a vibrant thread, a narrative element as potent as his life. It embodies the essence of his character, his courage, his acceptance of fate, and his indomitable spirit, characteristics that have etched Ragnar's name in the annals of history and legend.

Ragnar's death, much like his life, remains a subject of fascination and debate. It serves as a stark reminder that the line between history and myth is often blurred, the two elements entwining to create a compelling narrative. The death of Ragnar Lothbrok, whether a historical event or a mythic tale, remains a powerful symbol of the Viking Age, an enduring legacy of a man who was, in life and death, larger than life.

Chapter 17: The Fury of Sons

The death of Ragnar Lothbrok was far from the end of the saga. Instead, it was the fiery spark that ignited a furious retaliation from his sons. Their revenge was as profound and decisive as their father's exploits, leading to the further expansion of Viking influence across the European continent.

The Oath of Blood

Ragnar's death was not a silent event. The news of his demise at the hands of King Ælla, in a pit of venomous snakes, travelled across the North Sea, carried on the winds to the shores of Scandinavia. It reached the ears of Ragnar's sons, who had scattered across the Viking territories, each carving out his own legend.

It was a chilling moment, a test of their resolve and their commitment to their father's legacy. Yet, in the face of their personal loss, Ragnar's sons rallied together, bound by a shared purpose. They swore a blood oath, a sacred vow to avenge their father's death and bring ruin upon King Ælla. This was not just a pledge of retribution, but a testament to their unity, their shared lineage, and the embodiment of their father's indomitable spirit.

Gathering the Great Heathen Army

The task ahead was immense. King Ælla's forces were formidable, his defenses well-established. The sons of Ragnar, though seasoned warriors themselves, knew that vengeance would require more than their individual strengths. It would necessitate a show of force unparalleled in Viking history.

Thus began the gathering of the Great Heathen Army. This was not a mere assembly of warriors, but a symbol of Viking unity, a response to the injustice done to one of their greatest heroes. Men from all corners of the Viking territories joined the ranks, drawn by the call for justice and the allure of conquest. From the fjords of Norway to the shores of Denmark, the sons of Ragnar amassed a force that would make the kingdoms of England tremble.

The Fury Unleashed
Once assembled, the Great Heathen Army sailed for the shores of Northumbria. Their ships, like dark spectres on the horizon, signaled the onset of a storm that would engulf Ælla's kingdom. The revenge of Ragnar's sons was not a covert operation, but a sweeping, thunderous assault.

The Battle of York was the first significant encounter. The city's walls, a symbol of Northumbrian strength, were no match for the fury of the Viking invaders. They surged through the city, toppling defenses, razing buildings, and cutting down anyone who stood in their way. The city fell, but the sons of Ragnar were not yet satisfied. King Ælla, the object of their fury, was still at large.

The pursuit of Ælla was relentless. It was a manhunt fueled by vengeance, by the vision of their father dying in a pit of snakes. When Ælla was finally captured, the sons of Ragnar showed no mercy. In a savage display of poetic justice, they executed him using the blood eagle, a brutal ritual previously discussed in this saga. The man responsible for their father's death met an end as grisly as the one he had inflicted.

The Expansion of Viking Influence
With Ælla's death, the sons of Ragnar had fulfilled their oath. Yet, their conquest was not over. They had tasted victory, seen the power of their united force, and recognized the potential for greater glory. Their campaign extended beyond Northumbria, sweeping across the kingdoms of England. They raided monasteries, seized towns, and claimed territories, extending the sphere of Viking influence.

Ragnar's death had sparked a revolution. His sons, in their quest for revenge, had not only avenged their father but also cemented their own legacies. They were no longer just the sons of Ragnar Lothbrok; they were the embodiment of Viking power, the carriers of their father's spirit.

The fury of Ragnar's sons was a turning point in the Viking Age. It marked a shift in the dynamic between the Vikings and the kingdoms of England, a change in the balance of power. The Vikings were no longer just raiders appearing sporadically on foreign shores. They were a force to be reckoned with, a power that commanded respect and fear.

The Legacy of Revenge

In the wake of their furious retribution, Ragnar's sons left a significant impact on the historical landscape. Their deeds, driven by the desire for revenge, shaped the course of Viking history, setting the stage for future generations.

In avenging their father's death, they became figures of legend in their own right. Their actions were the subject of sagas, songs, and stories, passed down through the ages. They became symbols of courage, unity, and resolution, embodying the spirit of the Viking Age.

The fury of Ragnar's sons was more than an act of vengeance; it was a testament to their father's legacy. Through their deeds, they honored Ragnar's memory, carrying his spirit forward into the annals of Viking history.

In conclusion, the sons of Ragnar Lothbrok, united by the tragic death of their father, forged a path of revenge that forever shaped the Viking world. Their fury led to a transformation of Viking influence, bringing about a new era of Viking dominance and ushering in a chapter of history written in the language of power, vengeance, and conquest.

Chapter 18: Viking Expeditions and Settlements

Ragnar Lothbrok's exploits – along with those of his descendants – had a far-reaching influence on Viking expeditions and settlement patterns. His daring voyages, strategic battles, and notable sieges paved the way for extensive exploration, conquests, and colonies by the Vikings, particularly in regions such as England and parts of Eastern Europe.

The Seafaring Vikings

Viking expeditions were characterized by their maritime prowess and their far-reaching ship-bound explorations. These expeditions were not only carried out for the purpose of raiding, but they were also instrumental in establishing long-term settlements. The Vikings' superior seafaring skills and shipbuilding technology, as detailed earlier in the context of Ragnar's exploits, were key elements that facilitated their overseas excursions.

These expeditions were driven by a combination of several factors: the pursuit of wealth, the search for new farming lands due to population pressures in their homeland, and not to forget, the lust for glory and adventure inspired by legendary figures like Ragnar Lothbrok.

England: A New Viking Frontier

England was one of the primary destinations of these Viking expeditions. Following the successful raids and the eventual conquest led by Ragnar's sons, the Vikings began to see England not just as a land ripe for plunder, but also as a territory suitable for permanent settlement.

The creation of the Danelaw, a historical name given to the part of England where the laws of the Danes held sway, signified the Vikings' intent to stay. It was not a single area, but a collection of territories spread across England, each governed by Viking law. These areas witnessed a considerable influx of Viking settlers, who brought with them their culture, language, and way of life.

The Danelaw was more than just a territorial gain for the Vikings. It was a testament to their adaptability, their ability to not just conquer lands but also to cultivate and develop them. They established market towns, fostered trade, and introduced new farming techniques, thereby integrating themselves into the socio-economic fabric of the region.

Eastern Europe and the Varangians

Viking expeditions weren't just focused on the west. The east also held a strong allure, leading many Vikings to venture into territories that are now part of modern-day Russia, Ukraine, and Belarus. The Vikings who embarked on these eastern expeditions were often referred to as Varangians.

The Varangians explored and traversed the extensive river networks of Eastern Europe, establishing trade routes and settlements along the way. They engaged in commerce with the Byzantine Empire and the Arab kingdoms, trading goods like honey, wax, furs, and slaves.

These expeditions eventually led to the creation of powerful state entities, such as the Kievan Rus. The Vikings' influence in these areas was profound, contributing significantly to the cultural and political development of the region.

Impact of Ragnar and His Descendants
The influence of Ragnar Lothbrok and his descendants on Viking expeditions and settlements was substantial. Ragnar's successful raids, combined with the tales of his exploits, ignited a sense of adventure and ambition among the Vikings. It motivated them to undertake daring voyages and to conquer new lands.

Similarly, the actions of Ragnar's sons, particularly their revenge campaign against King Ælla and their subsequent establishment of the Danelaw, played a pivotal role in encouraging Viking settlement in England. Their exploits set a precedent for future generations of Vikings, showing them the possibilities that lay beyond their homeland.

In the east, while there isn't a direct connection to Ragnar and his sons, their spirit of exploration and conquest undoubtedly echoed in the journeys of the Varangians. The establishment of the Kievan Rus and other political entities in Eastern Europe bore the hallmarks of Viking tenacity and ambition, traits that were exemplified by Ragnar and his lineage.

In conclusion, the influence of Ragnar Lothbrok and his descendants significantly shaped the direction of Viking expeditions and their settlement patterns. Their deeds, woven into the sagas and legends of the Viking Age, played a crucial role in guiding the Vikings towards new frontiers, encouraging them to seek wealth, glory, and new homes beyond the seas. As such, the footprint of Ragnar and his descendants can be found in the Viking settlements that sprouted across England, as well as the trade routes and political entities established by the Varangians in Eastern Europe. Through their actions, the world of the Vikings expanded, and their impact on history became more profound.

Chapter 19: The Legend in Literature

Among the annals of history, Ragnar Lothbrok stands as a fascinating character, straddling the fine line between historical figure and legendary hero. His saga, largely disseminated through oral tradition, was eventually penned down in various forms of literature. Through sagas, skaldic poetry, and historical texts, Ragnar's story was perpetuated, his exploits embellished, and his legend immortalized.

Sagas: Ragnar's Epic Life Story

Sagas played a crucial role in preserving the legacy of Ragnar Lothbrok. A distinctly Nordic form of prose literature, sagas usually depicted historical events, legendary heroes, and mythical beings, weaving a rich tapestry of narrative that was both entertaining and educative.

"The Saga of Ragnar Lothbrok," or "Ragnarssona þáttr" in Old Norse, is the most comprehensive literary work focusing on Ragnar. This saga presented a grand narrative of his life, touching on his childhood, his daring exploits, his marriages, the birth and rise of his sons, and his gruesome death. It was not only a chronicle of events but also a reflection of the society and values of the Viking Age.

Ragnar's portrayal in the saga is that of an archetypal Viking hero: brave, cunning, and larger-than-life. From his audacious slaying of a dragon to his leadership during the siege of Paris, Ragnar exemplified the heroic virtues that were deeply admired in Norse culture. However, it's crucial to note that sagas often blended historical events with fictional elements, rendering Ragnar's character and deeds partly fantastical.

Skaldic Poetry: The Bard's Praise

Skaldic poetry was another medium through which Ragnar's legend was propagated. Skalds, or court poets, were esteemed figures in Norse society, tasked with composing and performing verses in honor of kings and heroes. These verses were characterized by their complex metrical patterns, elaborate kennings (metaphorical expressions), and rich allusions to mythology and history.

Ragnar, as a prominent figure of his time, was a popular subject of skaldic verse. While most of these compositions did not survive in their entirety, fragments referenced in sagas and historical texts provide glimpses of how Ragnar was perceived and praised. For instance, verses lauding his bravery, wisdom, and martial prowess were common, reinforcing the image of Ragnar as an extraordinary warrior-king.

Historical Chronicles: The Outsider's Perspective

Beyond sagas and poetry, Ragnar's presence is also found in several historical chronicles, though often indirectly and in a less flamboyant manner. These chronicles, mostly written by Christian monks in England and France, provide an outsider's perspective on Ragnar and the Vikings.

Frankish annals, such as "The Annals of Saint-Bertin," mention a "Reginherus" or "Ragnarius" leading a Viking siege of Paris in 845, a name considered by some scholars to be a Latinized version of Ragnar. Similarly, English texts like the "Anglo-Saxon Chronicle" allude to a great Viking army, which, according to the Norse sagas, was led by Ragnar's sons to avenge their father's death.

While these records corroborate certain elements of Ragnar's saga, their perspective often varies significantly from the Norse narratives. The Christian chroniclers generally portrayed the Vikings as brutal raiders and heathens, with their leaders, possibly including Ragnar, depicted as ruthless invaders. This contrast adds another layer to the complex character of Ragnar, highlighting the dichotomy between his vilification as an invader and his veneration as a hero.

Ragnar's Enduring Legacy in Literature

The literary representations of Ragnar Lothbrok – be it in sagas, poetry, or historical texts – have undeniably shaped our understanding of the man and his myth. They have crafted a multifaceted portrayal of Ragnar: a hero to his people, a scourge to his enemies, a dragon slayer, a king, a father, and a legend.

Through these works, Ragnar has transcended the boundaries of time and place. He is not merely a figure of the past but an enduring symbol embodying the ethos of the Viking Age. His saga, fraught with peril, glory, and tragedy, continues to capture the imagination of readers and historians alike.

Yet, the Ragnar of literature should be approached with a discerning eye. The confluence of fact and fiction in these works blurs the line between the historical Ragnar and the mythical Lothbrok. As such, extracting the man from the myth is a challenging, if not impossible, task. Nevertheless, the uncertainty surrounding Ragnar's historicity does not diminish the cultural and historical significance of his legend.

In essence, the portrayal of Ragnar Lothbrok in literature – whether accurate or embellished – is a testament to the enduring fascination with his character. Ragnar, in his literary incarnations, serves as a window into the Viking Age, offering insights into its social values, beliefs, and worldview. As we delve into these tales and verses, we come closer to understanding the man behind the legend and the culture that produced such a captivating saga.

Chapter 20: The Viking Hero

In the annals of history, certain figures rise to legendary status, embodying the virtues and values of their cultures. For the Vikings, one such figure was Ragnar Lothbrok. His exploits, both real and embellished, defined the archetype of the Viking hero, a character woven into the fabric of Norse society. In this chapter, we shall dissect this construct, using Ragnar as our prime example.

Bravery: The Valor of a Warrior
First and foremost, bravery stood at the core of a Viking hero. Courage in the face of danger, both on the battlefield and in daring adventures, was a trait deeply admired in Norse society. Ragnar's life, as narrated in sagas and poems, was a testament to this virtue.

Whether it was facing a dragon singlehandedly, raiding foreign lands against formidable defenses, or leading his men into battle, Ragnar repeatedly demonstrated his courage. Such fearlessness was not reckless abandon but a deliberate choice to confront danger, emphasizing the Viking belief in predestination and the heroic pursuit of glory.

Wisdom: The Cunning Strategist

In addition to physical courage, wisdom was an integral attribute of a Viking hero. This wisdom often manifested in strategic cunning, shrewd diplomacy, and insightful understanding of the world. These qualities were as critical as physical prowess, often marking the difference between a common warrior and a renowned hero.

Ragnar's legend offers several instances of such wisdom. His strategy to defeat the dragon by using a suit of fur and tar showcased his inventive approach to challenges. His successful raids, notably the siege of Paris, underscored his strategic brilliance. Furthermore, his ability to navigate the intricate web of Viking politics to ascend to power, as recounted in the sagas, illustrated his political acumen.

Honor: The Code of Conduct

The Viking hero was also defined by an ingrained sense of honor, adhering to a code of conduct that governed warfare, interactions with others, and personal conduct. This code, interwoven with the warrior ethos of the Vikings, encompassed principles of loyalty, honesty, and respect for the gods.

Ragnar Lothbrok, in his heroic persona, displayed an unwavering commitment to these values. He was depicted as a loyal friend and a just ruler, often stepping in to settle disputes and uphold justice. His respect for the gods and adherence to Viking rituals illustrated his commitment to religious duties. Even in his purported death in the snake pit,

Ragnar faced his fate with dignity, adhering to the Viking belief of dying a 'good death'.

Legacy: The Prolific Progenitor

One of the ways a Viking hero's greatness was measured was through his offspring. A strong, brave, and wise hero was expected to produce sons who could carry forward his legacy. In Ragnar's case, this aspect of heroism was strikingly pronounced.

Ragnar's sons, each a formidable figure in their own right, were central characters in the continuation of Ragnar's saga. They avenged his death, led the Great Heathen Army, and became legends in their own right. Thus, Ragnar's legacy was not only his personal achievements but also the exploits of his sons, underlining the Viking perception of heroism as an enduring lineage.

Charisma: The Magnetic Leader

Charisma was a subtle yet critical element of the Viking hero. The ability to inspire, lead, and earn the respect of others was a trait that distinguished a hero from an ordinary warrior. This charisma was often a blend of personal qualities: physical strength, eloquence, generosity, and a certain magnetism that attracted followers.

Ragnar, in his legendary form, was undoubtedly a charismatic figure. He rallied men to join him in daring raids, navigated the volatile realm of Viking politics, and became a figure of inspiration in Norse society. His charisma not only propelled his personal journey from a warrior to a king but also facilitated the consolidation of his legacy, enabling his story to endure through the centuries.

In conclusion, the construct of the Viking hero was multifaceted, blending physical valor, intellectual prowess, honor, legacy, and charisma. Ragnar Lothbrok, as depicted in Norse literature, embodied these attributes, serving as a quintessential Viking hero. His legend, however mythical, offered a lens to understand the Viking ethos and their perception of heroism.

The Viking hero, much like the era itself, was complex and paradoxical, capable of both great violence and deep wisdom, driven by a pursuit of honor and glory that often led to perilous adventures. And at the heart of this paradox stood Ragnar Lothbrok – the Dragon Slayer, the Sea-King, the legend – a hero who continues to epitomize the Viking Age, centuries after his time.

Chapter 21: Vikings and the Christian World

For the Viking era, a significant theme was the cultural, religious, and political clashes between the pagan Norse and the Christian world. While raiding Christian territories for wealth and power, the Vikings faced a civilization with differing beliefs and practices. This interaction had profound implications, eventually contributing to the Christianization of the Viking world. In this chapter, we'll investigate these complex relationships through the lens of Ragnar Lothbrok's encounters with Christian kings and societies.

A Pagan Warrior in a Christian Land

The expansion of the Viking Age coincided with the era of Christian consolidation in Europe. Vikings, like Ragnar Lothbrok, found themselves interacting frequently with Christian societies, either as traders or as raiders. The clash of these two contrasting worldviews set the stage for fascinating interactions and conflicts.

Ragnar, according to the sagas, was no stranger to the Christian world. As a sea-king who led raids in foreign lands, he faced Christian kingdoms that defended their territories and their faith against pagan intruders. His raid of Paris in 845, where he faced the Christian king Charles the Bald, was a prominent example of these interactions.

During these encounters, Ragnar would have witnessed the Christian rituals, symbols, and practices quite different from his own pagan traditions. However, these experiences did not sway him from his Norse beliefs, at least according to the sagas. He remained a staunch follower of the old gods, often invoking them in his exploits and attributing his victories to their favor.

Vikings: Raiders or Traders?
While the image of Vikings as brutal raiders is etched in historical consciousness, they were also prolific traders. Viking trading routes spanned from their Scandinavian homeland to places as far as Byzantium and Baghdad. Christian kingdoms were part of these trade networks, with exchanges going beyond material goods to include cultural and ideological influences.

It is plausible that Ragnar, in addition to his famed raids, may have participated in these trading activities. His interactions with the Christian world would not have been limited to the battlefield. He might have witnessed the contrast of bustling Christian marketplaces to his native trading towns, encountered foreign goods, and experienced foreign customs and languages.

These trading interactions were significant, not just for their economic value, but for the cultural exchange they enabled. Over time, they played a crucial role in reshaping the Viking's understanding and perception of the Christian world.

Clashing Worldviews: Paganism and Christianity

At the heart of the Viking and Christian world's encounters was a fundamental clash of worldviews: the Norse pagan beliefs and Christian monotheism. Ragnar, being a fervent follower of the Norse gods, would have viewed the Christian beliefs through his pagan lens. His gods were embodiments of nature and war, revered through rituals and sacrifices, quite divergent from the Christian concept of a single omnipotent God worshipped in churches.

Yet, despite these stark differences, elements of syncretism emerged as the two cultures interacted. Some Vikings adopted Christian symbols alongside their pagan ones, perhaps as amulets or markers of prestige. While there's no evidence that Ragnar himself did this, these practices indicate the complex and evolving relationship between the pagan Vikings and the Christian world.

The Beginnings of Conversion

The Viking Age also saw the beginnings of the Christianization of the Norse. Although Ragnar's lifetime, according to the sagas, predates the large-scale conversions, the seeds of this transformation were sown in this era.

Ragnar's interaction with Christian kings may have included witnessing some of his fellow Vikings choose to convert to Christianity, either willingly for political alliances or forcefully upon defeat. Such scenarios represent the simmering religious tensions of the time, the subtle shifts in Viking religiosity, and the increasing Christian influence.

The Christianization process was not an overnight event but a gradual and often violent transformation spanning over centuries. In the time of Ragnar, the Christian world was not just an adversary or a destination for raids, but also an agent of cultural and religious change.

Ragnar Lothbrok and the Christian World: An Intricate Dance
Reflecting on Ragnar's encounters with the Christian world provides a glimpse into the broader dynamics of Viking-Christian relations. His raids brought him face-to-face with Christian defenses, both military and spiritual. His probable involvement in trade facilitated cultural exchanges, and his witness to the burgeoning Christian influence marked the nascent shifts in Viking religious landscape.

Through Ragnar's lens, we perceive a complex and intricate dance between the pagan Vikings and the Christian world, characterized by conflict, cooperation, and co-evolution. These interactions, loaded with contrasts and contradictions, set the stage for significant transformations in Viking society, with implications that echoed far beyond the lifetime of the legendary Ragnar Lothbrok.

Chapter 22: From Saga to Screen

The enduring fascination with the Viking era and its larger-than-life characters like Ragnar Lothbrok has found its way into the modern consciousness, not only through books and historical texts but also through popular media. One of the most influential portrayals of Ragnar and his saga can be seen in the widely-acclaimed television series "Vikings."

The Birth of "Vikings"
"Vikings," created by Michael Hirst, first premiered in 2013 on the History Channel. Set in the backdrop of the Viking Age, the show aimed to depict the Viking world's realities and myths and shed light on their complex society. Among its central characters was Ragnar Lothbrok, portrayed by actor Travis Fimmel.

The show's creation was a result of the growing global interest in Viking history and culture, spurred by archaeological discoveries, academic research, and a renewed fascination with Norse mythology. Ragnar, with his legendary exploits and enigmatic personality, naturally became the series' anchor, capturing the viewers' imagination.

Ragnar Lothbrok: The Screen Hero

On-screen, Ragnar Lothbrok is presented as a legendary Viking chieftain and explorer, a curious and ambitious man determined to discover and raid new lands. True to the sagas, he is shown as a devoted follower of the Norse gods, a fearless warrior, a shrewd strategist, and a loving, if sometimes flawed, father and husband.

While the historical accuracy of the show can be debated, its depiction of Ragnar is undoubtedly compelling. Travis Fimmel's nuanced performance captures the complexity of the character, from his burning ambition and intellectual curiosity to his personal struggles and contradictions.

The Saga on Screen: Fact or Fiction?
"Vikings" navigates the delicate balance between historical fact and the mythical sagas, creating an entertaining yet informative narrative. It incorporates many of the legendary tales associated with Ragnar, such as his dragon-slaying feat, his raids in England and France, his marriages to Lagertha and Aslaug, and his eventual fall.

However, the show also takes creative liberties in its storytelling, sometimes deviating from both historical record and the sagas. For instance, characters like Rollo and Floki, while based on real historical figures, are woven into Ragnar's narrative in ways not supported by the sagas or historical texts. Some events, like the raids on Paris, are not temporally accurate.

Despite these departures, the essence of the Ragnar Lothbrok legend and the spirit of the Viking Age are retained. The show paints a vivid, albeit dramatized, picture of Viking society, their customs, beliefs, politics, and their interaction with the Christian world.

"Vikings" Influence on Modern Perception of Ragnar and the Viking Age

Since its premiere, "Vikings" has had a profound impact on the modern perception of the Viking Age and characters like Ragnar Lothbrok. The series has introduced millions worldwide to the sagas and legends of this fascinating era and has kindled interest in Viking history and culture.

Ragnar Lothbrok, as portrayed in the series, has become a symbol of the Viking warrior spirit, a representation of both their martial prowess and their intellectual curiosity. He embodies the adventurous seafarer, the fearless warrior, the devoted pagan, the wise leader, and the flawed human, making the legendary figure accessible and relatable to the modern audience.

In the process, the show has helped dispel some persistent stereotypes about Vikings, presenting them not just as brutal raiders, but as complex individuals living in a complex society. It highlights their sophistication in navigation, shipbuilding, law and governance, and their intricate relationship with the wider world.

Ragnar Lothbrok: An Enduring Legend

From ancient sagas to the modern television screen, the legend of Ragnar Lothbrok continues to captivate and intrigue. The "Vikings" series, despite its departures from historical and saga-based narratives, brings Ragnar's legend to life in a way that is both engaging and informative.

Ragnar's portrayal in "Vikings" serves as a testament to the enduring allure of his legend. It is a reminder that the tales we tell, whether through ancient sagas or television dramas, shape our understanding of history and the people who made it.

Through its complex, charismatic central character, "Vikings" invites its audience to explore the fascinating world of the Viking Age, sparking interest and curiosity about this unique chapter of human history.

In conclusion, the journey of Ragnar Lothbrok from saga to screen is a fascinating tale in itself, reflective of our enduring fascination with the Viking Age and its iconic figures. "Vikings" is not just a television drama; it's a modern vessel carrying ancient tales, captivating new generations and ensuring the legend of Ragnar Lothbrok lives on. As we look back at the many faces and tales of Ragnar, we realize that his story, like the story of the Viking Age itself, is an ever-evolving tapestry of fact, fiction, and timeless fascination.

Chapter 23: Debunking the Myths

In the spectrum of our historical understanding, myths and misconceptions often run parallel with the facts. The life and times of the Viking warrior king, Ragnar Lothbrok, are no exception. In this chapter, we will peel back the veil of folklore, dispelling some of the enduring myths about Vikings and examining Ragnar's life as a litmus test of Viking reality versus enduring fantasy.

Myth 1: Vikings Wore Horned Helmets
When we think of a Viking warrior, the first image that often comes to mind is of a tall, muscular figure clad in leather or chainmail, a sword or an axe in hand, and a horned helmet perched on his head. This iconic representation, however, is a fabrication. In reality, there is no archaeological or historical evidence to suggest that Vikings wore horned helmets in battle.

Horned helmets were indeed found in Scandinavia, but they date back to the Bronze Age, long before the Viking Age. They were likely used for ceremonial purposes and not for combat. The image of a Viking in a horned helmet is a product of 19th-century Romanticism, specifically, Richard Wagner's opera "Der Ring des Nibelungen," where the costume designer chose to adorn the Viking characters with horned helmets. Thus, while Ragnar Lothbrok and his fellow warriors were undoubtedly fearsome in battle, they achieved their victories without the assistance of horned headgear.

Myth 2: Vikings Were Only Raiders and Plunderers

The image of the Viking as a marauding raider, descending upon unsuspecting villages to pillage and destroy, is deeply entrenched in popular imagination. While it's true that Vikings did engage in raiding - and Ragnar Lothbrok is renowned for his exploits on the seas - this was not their only, or even primary, activity.

Vikings were also accomplished traders, navigating trade routes from Scandinavia to the Middle East, exchanging goods like furs, ivory, and amber for silks, spices, and precious metals. They were skilled craftsmen, with their intricate metalwork, carvings, and shipbuilding techniques testifying to a complex and cultured society. They were explorers, who, according to the sagas, reached as far as North America, several centuries before Christopher Columbus. They were farmers, who cultivated the lands in their homelands and in the new territories they settled.

Ragnar's life encapsulates this multi-faceted identity of the Vikings. He was a warrior, but also a ruler who administered laws and managed his kingdom. His legendary raids did not define the totality of his existence, nor did they represent the sole occupation of the Viking people.

Myth 3: Vikings Were Uncivilized Barbarians

The violent raids conducted by the Vikings and their reputation for fierceness in battle have contributed to the stereotype of Vikings as uncivilized barbarians. However, a closer look at their society reveals a much more nuanced picture.

The Vikings had a complex societal structure, with a legal system that included a kind of representative assembly known as a 'thing.' They believed in a sophisticated pantheon of gods and engaged in intricate religious rituals. Their artistic expression, seen in their intricate carvings and ornate jewelry, points to a rich cultural life.

In the sagas, Ragnar Lothbrok is not merely a brute force; he's often portrayed as a clever strategist and a wise ruler. His victories are as much a result of his intellect as his physical prowess, underlining that Vikings were not mere savages but capable of advanced tactical thinking and governance.

Myth 4: All Vikings Were Blond

The image of a Viking is often that of a tall, blond-haired, blue-eyed warrior. While it's true that blond hair was considered ideal in Viking society - to the extent that some Vikings bleached their hair - the Vikings were a diverse group.

Scandinavia was a crossroads of cultures, with people coming from all across Europe and Asia, bringing with them a mix of genetic traits. So, Vikings would have ranged in appearance from blond to brown or red-haired, with a variety of eye colors.

Ragnar himself, as described in some accounts, had dark hair, demonstrating that the blond Viking is more stereotype than standard.

Myth 5: Viking Women Were Subservient

While it's true that Viking society was patriarchal, women in the Viking Age had more rights and freedoms compared to women in many other societies of the same period. They could own property, request a divorce, and serve as a 'volva,' a woman who was believed to possess prophetic powers and held a high status in society.

The sagas even speak of shieldmaidens - women who chose the path of the warrior, such as Lagertha, Ragnar's first wife, who is portrayed as a formidable fighter in her own right. While the extent to which shieldmaidens existed is debated among scholars, their presence in the sagas suggests that Viking women were not merely passive players in their society.

Ragnar Lothbrok's life, as recorded in the sagas, is intertwined with such influential women, underlining their integral role in Viking society.

Debunking these myths does not diminish the allure of the Viking Age or the legend of Ragnar Lothbrok. On the contrary, it brings into sharper focus the true richness and complexity of this fascinating period and the people who lived through it. Their world was not a realm of fantasy, but a reality that was equally remarkable - a tapestry woven from the threads of fact and fiction, history and legend, creating a story as enduring as the tale of Ragnar Lothbrok himself.

Chapter 24: Ragnar's Hourglass

As the hourglass of our journey through Ragnar's life reaches its final grains, it is time for reflection, contemplation, and some concluding thoughts on this legendary figure. We stand now at the confluence of history, myth, and legend, the waters of truth, and the currents of fantasy, intermingling to form the powerful stream of Ragnar's narrative that has flowed down through the centuries.

The sands of Ragnar's hourglass have been speckled with blood and gold, touched by the grit of battle, and the lustre of triumph. They have been tempered by stormy seas, the whispers of the gods, and the echoes of love and kinship. Ragnar Lothbrok, the Viking warrior king, straddles this ever-shifting realm, as much a man as he is a myth, a beacon of the Viking age that continues to illuminate the darkened corners of history.

An Icon of the Viking Age
Ragnar Lothbrok is indelibly linked to the Viking Age. He epitomizes its valor, resilience, and thirst for exploration, embodying the Viking spirit in all its tumultuous grandeur. His life, as told in the sagas, is a microcosm of this extraordinary period in history – an era that witnessed the

blossoming of seafaring, trading, and raiding capabilities of a people who left an indelible mark on the world.

However, Ragnar's legacy is not just about external conquests and geographical expansion. It's also about the inner horizons of cultural evolution and societal dynamics. His story captures the ethos of the Vikings – their values, their beliefs, their societal structure, and their ways of life. He provides us with a window into a society that was far more nuanced and sophisticated than commonly portrayed.

Ragnar's saga is a testament to the richness of oral tradition and the power of storytelling, which served as the lifeblood of Viking culture. In these narratives, Ragnar emerges as a heroic archetype, a figure who encapsulates the virtues, ideals, and aspirations of his people.

The Interplay of History and Legend

Ragnar's story rests on the delicate edge between history and legend. While historical records provide scant information about him, his presence in sagas and poems is vivid and indelible. This duality, the absence in one domain and the abundance in another, only adds to the enigma of Ragnar.

Did he truly slay a dragon, besiege Paris, and meet his end in a pit of snakes? We may never fully untangle fact from fiction. However, the lack of historical clarity does not diminish Ragnar's cultural significance. If anything, it amplifies his stature as a figure who transcends the bounds of history to occupy the hallowed realms of legend and folklore.

Ragnar's narrative underscores the richness of Viking oral tradition, where the lines between history and myth were often blurred. The sagas were not merely tales of grandeur and adventure; they were a lens through which the Vikings understood their world and their place in it. In this sense, Ragnar's story is as much about the people who recounted his saga as it is about the legendary figure himself.

Ragnar's Enduring Influence
Ragnar's saga has traversed the vast ocean of time, carried forward by the tides of oral and written tradition, inspiring and captivating generations. His life, woven from threads of history and embellished with the embroidery of legend, continues to resonate in contemporary consciousness.

His influence extends beyond the confines of historical texts and sagas; it permeates popular culture, inspiring novels, TV shows, and films. Ragnar has become a symbol, an icon of the Vikings that continues to fascinate and enthrall. He has evolved into a cultural construct that represents our fascination with the Viking age and its enduring appeal.

It's not just the man who fascinates us, but the era he represents—an era of exploration, courage, and cultural ferment. Ragnar's story encapsulates the essence of the Viking spirit – their bravery, their thirst for adventure, their resilience in the face of adversity.

This is the true power of Ragnar's narrative. It bridges the gulf between past and present, serving as a conduit that connects us to a time long past. His story invites us to reflect on our own societies, our own values, and our own understanding of the world.

The sands in Ragnar's hourglass may have run their course, but the echoes of his saga continue to reverberate. He remains a potent symbol of the Viking Age, a figure who captures our imagination and engages our intellect. His life continues to serve as a prism, refracting the light of a distant era into a spectrum of colors that continues to fascinate and inspire.

In the final analysis, Ragnar Lothbrok, whether man or myth, has achieved a form of immortality, living on in the sagas that sing his praises and in the minds of those who recount his story. His hourglass may have run its course, but the sands of his time continue to sparkle in the annals of history, a reminder of a man and an era that continue to shape our understanding of the Viking Age. As the curtains of our saga draw to a close, one thing is abundantly clear: the legend of Ragnar Lothbrok, the Viking Warrior King, is far from over.

Printed in Great Britain
by Amazon